THE ACCUMULATION EFFECT

THE ACCUMULATION EFFECT

How to Change Yourself for the Better

To you Sammi
The universe is always ready to hear your dreams!

Stephen A. Oliver

Steve ☺

STELLAR ★ BOOKS

Published in 2017 by

Stellar Books LLP
1 Birchdale
St Mary's Road
Bowdon
Cheshire
WA14 2PW, UK.

E: info@stellarbooks.co.uk
W: www.stellarbooks.co.uk
T: 0161 928 8273
Tw: @stellarbooksllp

ISBN: 978-1-910275-16-0

A copy of this book is available in the British Library.

www.stephenaoliver.com

www.theaccumulationeffect.com

Designed by Stephen A. Oliver

Typeset in Calibri and Century Gothic.

I want to dedicate this book to my mother and father, Irene and Richard Oliver.

They unknowingly created an environment for me that allowed me to be me. I was fed, safe and allowed to experiment with what I wanted to do, without judgement. Thank you for my life, for the sacrifices you made to allow it to unfold and the brave decisions that you made to give me the space and time to grow. My older brother and my younger sister also benefited from this. Although we were freer spirits than perhaps would be considered a good idea, we did find our own lives became what we mostly wanted. That freedom gave us our character that we now enjoy. I love you both.

Stephen

Contents

Acknowledgements

Just writing this book has had an accumulative effect on me. I had not planned to publish it and was just adding bits to it over the years. I hoped that for me it would be a reminder of the positivity of writing my ideas down and reflecting on them.

As I could have predicted, it has become more than the initial plan. I still keep adding to it now. It was useful when I got off track, has been useful for friends and family and now I find myself wanting it to be useful for as many people as I can reach out to.

The book itself is a testament to the very title. The long-term effect has been positive for me and some others too. It has helped me reach out to people like Patricia C. Byron, my publisher, who has kept me focused to make it happen. I may never have met her otherwise.

It has also had a delightful effect on my work colleagues, family and friends. The close ones who know my limitations are perhaps taken aback by its very existence. As am I.

This has lifted my thinking towards bigger and better projects. My long suffering PA Helen, knows how hard it is to keep me working in the right direction, and I will be forever grateful for her patience and tenacity.

My wife Tracey with whom I have decided to enforce many decisions on has been a sounding board, critic and moral compass for many of my wild plans. Goodness knows why she is able to stick at it with me.

My daughters, Zoë and Zara now have an example of why little steps towards big goals are so exciting and how they enhance your life.

Another very important person in my life is my incredibly loyal, disciplined and effort orientated friend David. I have nicknamed him 'Action Man' due to always being the one who takes action and gets me to do so too when often I wouldn't or thought I couldn't.

His unique ability to get people to take action has had such an effect on my life I can truly say I have a better one because of him. Taking action is the seed of accomplishment and change. *The Accumulation Effect* was born from it. Thank you David.

"A journey of a thousand miles begins with a single step."

Chinese proverb

Introduction

In 1985, I came across a book called *The Magic of Thinking Big* by David J. Schwartz. Although much of the content at the time seemed to pass me by, it started a process; a commitment within me to change myself for the better on a long-term, ongoing basis. Even today it amazes me how much of the book I seem to remember and just how much of it I have absorbed into my daily life. Some of Schwartz's suggestions I adopted then have become lifelong habits now.

Take for example Schwartz's instruction to walk 25 percent faster. Average people live average lives and have an average walk. It seemed almost silly to me back then and I even ridiculed it on a number of occasions. Now, many years later, I find I walk much faster and for the very reasons quoted in the book: walking faster suggests urgency, the need to be taken more seriously and it certainly makes me feel more confident, as if I have a greater sense of purpose.

My conclusion from this and many of Schwartz's suggestions is relatively simple: that what you are exposed to eventually has an effect on your outcomes. Take smoking for example. When you are young it seems to have no effect at all, apart from making you smell bad to non-smokers. Your health seems the same and cancer doesn't even seem to be a threat. After years of smoking, the exposure and effects becomes more evident: less stamina, shortness of breath, a tired look that you don't recognise in yourself. There are lines on your face that weren't there before and stains on your fingers.... and these are just a few of the examples which I could mention. What seemed like just fun became a habit. You spend hundreds of pounds on them monthly and you discover that, after 30 years, your health has severely deteriorated and you've spent years' worth of income on something that is now threatening your very existence. What's more is that, because you smoke, your kids think it's okay to smoke too... and so the cycle continues.

Consider too the financial cost: in today's terms, you could spend £1,600 purchasing cigarettes. That means you had to earn £2,000 a year before tax to purchase them. That £1,600 a year could have been saved and, if it achieved only five percent a year growth, it could have become, over a period of 30 years, a healthy £111,615!

But the real tragedy is the fact that smoking is no longer just about the amount of money spent. The real cost of your decisions, is the irreplaceable loss of health and the effect on your relationships as well as the impact on others' lives.

Everything we do affects
everything we become

The example of the smoker is one that helps explain the point with devastating accuracy. But, even with these facts easily available, people still choose to sabotage their future.

This book is about why and what to do about it. It's about being aware of the true effect of your actions and having the tools to make the type of decisions that will help you live longer, make more of the opportunities that come your way and, most of all, be a better you. Being aware that all you touch and think and see and do can either taint or enhance your life in the future, has a very sobering effect.

Knowing that if you laugh the whole world laughs with you also has an element of truth that is just impossible to ignore yet is a fundamental which can bring change to the whole outcome of your life. Smile and others smile. Yawn and others yawn. **Everything** has an accumulative effect.

If you want to be a better you, then first analyse what it is around you that is influencing you now. Are you reading Stephen King or The Bible? Do you sleep all you can or exercise to give yourself more energy? Do the people you associate with mostly spend their time in the pub or are they actively doing something worthwhile such as teaching, creating, or even listening to someone who needs it. Chances are, whatever activity you spend most time doing, you are. Those you spend time with reflect that and influence you.

The amazing thing is that you do have a choice on what and who you become. You do have the ability to control nearly all the things in your life. The things that you can't control are the issues that you have to manage. Bad things happen. What you do about them and how you handle them, is your choice.

When you're in the pub and complain about having had a bad day, your friends will say, "Don't worry! Have a beer." "Have enough beer to stop thinking about it and you'll have a better day tomorrow."

If you believe that whole-heartedly then put this book down now. It is not for you yet. You could however decide that this bad day has some great examples of what not to do or what to avoid in future or just something to remind yourself of what a good day is. Better still, you could learn or train to make sure that you never get into that type of trap, trouble, disaster, or misfortune again.

Sometimes life throws a curved ball that takes years to get over or just changes you forever, like cancer, death of a loved one or the loss of sight or a limb. Regardless of the shock, and the difficulties you may have to overcome, you have the choice of how to react. The accumulation of your habits to that point will more often than not determine what shape that reaction will be. When breast cancer struck my younger sister, I was amazed at her positive attitude towards dealing with it. Since having two mastectomies and reconstruction surgery, in her words, she now "enjoys the ownership of the breasts of a nineteen year old."

Your external influences, your thought processes, what you read, who you hang out with, what you eat, and how you live your life, have a massive influence on the outcome of most of your life.

Your self-image is built up of the little pieces that make you what and who you are today. Each decision, negative thought, wasted day, lie, over indulgence, stray thought - even how often you clean your teeth - continues to craft the YOU that you are. The very root of the word character is from the description of chiselling a piece of wood. A sculptor will chisel away all the parts of a block that isn't wanted in order to expose the part he does. Just like your character, you can remove what you don't want.

Edward Lorenz, a meteorologist at the Massachusetts Institute of Technology coined the phrase *'The Butterfly Effect'* when trying to explain the chaos theory. He touched on an explanation for almost all of our lives' events, in my view.

> *"Character is the result of hundreds and hundreds of choices you make that gradually turn who you are, at any given moment, into who you want to be."*
>
> *Jim Rohn*

Let me, in this book, take you through a process that will change your life for the better. Share it with a good friend, family members - both young and old - and then accumulate habits that will enhance your life and change the outcome of your future in the most positive way imaginable.

I want to take you on a journey of examples of accumulated results that reflect on outcomes so obvious you'll wonder why you needed to read a book to discover it.

I want to help you to choose to be the best YOU you can be. I want to help you stack as much in your favour as you can; to be the exceptional individual you are but in a magnified form.

Ask yourself, what is unique and great about you? Is it hidden, on full show or have you yet to even think about it. Starting with your health let me help you discover a great, happy and powerful, YOU.

"Physical fitness is not only one of the most important keys to a healthy body, it is the basis of dynamic and creative intellectual activity."

John F. Kennedy

CHAPTER 1

Health

Let's be blunt and say up front, if you're born to parents who are five feet tall, it's likely you'll only ever be five feet tall. Unless one of your ancestors were much taller, chances are you'll not be much different to your parents.

Most of what we inherit in physical terms is fixed. However, what a five foot person can do is remarkable. Given the right environment, opportunities and drive, this person can achieve outstanding things and may find a chance to flourish *because* of his or her height.

Much of our ability has a limit....not always ones that we may think of though. An obvious limit is that we couldn't last long under water without a support system. We couldn't re-grow a limb that has been cut off or build a pyramid on our own in a day.....yet. However, with the accumulation of training, education and guidance, we could train ourselves to last five minutes or more under water. We could use a prosthetic limb so well that others wouldn't notice we were without a leg. A skilled site manager could arrange for a dam to be built in less than a year without having lifted a single brick or poured a bucket of concrete.

Why then does someone with developed skills make life seem so much easier than the lazy person who does as little as possible, who then blames everyone else for their misfortune? The accumulation of skills took us from apes to rulers of this planet. Even with basic skills, a child can survive in a West African slum where life is very challenging. So why do we act with such complacency, particularly in relation to our health?

Joe has been a good friend of mine for many years and is a very intelligent man. His love of music took him to the heights of knowledge in band culture and themed music that many of his friends admired. He has a passion for getting to know every record, band member, songwriter and musician in his chosen specialised field. His accumulated knowledge is outstanding. People choose to contact him for information and opinions. People who work in the same industry who should know it all and are paid to do so, call Joe for advice and tips and confirmation of history. He is a legend. That knowledge and passion has served him well and he knows he will always be able to learn more and this spurs him on.

However, he never paid any attention to his health, smoked like a chimney, drank like a fish, slept very little, ignored his wife except for sex and ate only when he could remember to and then it was usually poor quality, unhealthy food.

Now let me ask you. By the time he was 44 years old, do you think you could describe Joe's life? The obvious details are: health poor, overweight and quite smelly. The decline in his wellbeing had slowed his learning down but not enough so you'd notice. But what of his wife? You guessed it, long gone. His kids? Don't really know him. His friends? They changed a lot over the years; they mostly got fed up with his self-abuse and bored with the one-track conversation which always revolved around music, so they just started to distance themselves from him.

Now here's the very obvious question: could any of this have been foreseen? Of course. If you eat a chocolate bar a day instead of an apple a day then you will almost certainly be different in 20 years' time. Is it that simple? Yes. So why doesn't it stop us from doing the self-defeating stuff?

My only answers to date are firstly it's easier not to do what you should or avoid the stuff you shouldn't touch. Secondly it's a willingness to ignore the small stuff, which seem too small to be significant at the time. The really big stuff like whether to cheat on your partner or kill your neighbour after an argument is a bit more immediate.

Addictions take control of you, one event at a time. The repetition of a good or poor habit makes it difficult to change. It makes sense to weave good habits into your life. Be addicted to positive things.

We can often set a path or trait when we are young that stays with us for the rest of our lives. Consider this an example of the accumulation effect. Smoking or jogging? Drinking alcohol or health drinks? You are the one to choose.

This is the crux of my point in this whole book:

> It's the distance between the event and the effect that causes the apathy.

Let me explain: because it is a long time between your first chocolate bar and the doctor telling you that unless you cut down on the sweet stuff you're likely to have a heart attack, that we can ignore the accumulation effect. But it's bigger than that. Our whole culture is built around what we can get away with.

Do you remember when the Coalition forces liberated Iraq? The mob element took over and looting became widespread to such an extent that they robbed the hospitals of all sorts of life-saving equipment. I had a vision at the time of an ordinary Iraqi sitting in his breeze-block whitewashed apartment with an incubator he'd just stolen from the hospital and thinking, 'What the heck do I do with this now?' Group dynamics had taken over and he'd decided to go along and got carried away with his actions and stole the first thing he could get away with. He didn't think at the time 'What shall I do with the incubator?' He just thought 'I can get away with this.' It is hard to resist.

Imagine if you would that a chap goes to a hardware store and takes five items to the till. The checkout girl misses one of the items off and he notices it but pays the lower amount because he can easily blame her if he gets caught. He's just saved himself a few pounds and no one's the wiser. No risk no effort, he just took advantage of the opportunity that arose.

The accumulation effect has a long-term view of course. The cashier often made this mistake and just didn't care if this happened even when she noticed she'd done it. This casualness became entrenched and happened in many areas of her life. One day she was too casual with her own young daughter at the river's edge and the little girl fell in. Those lost seconds before she realised her mistake caused her daughter to drown. Too casual to the point of negligent? Yes perhaps. A lethargy built up over years of complacency. The accumulation effect in its negative form.

The chap who got away with the item thought that next time he came into the shop he'd try to get away with a few more expensive items and made a beeline for the same checkout girl.

Of course given the same opportunity to miss a few items still in the trolley that should have been scanned was simple and easy enough. Our customer decided that this could be fun to try in all walks of life and takes it several steps further. Then having stolen from a jewellers a few years later, got caught. The criminal record set him back so far that he never held a decent job again.

All this is unnecessary when you consider that a few common sayings are wisdom enough; like *Avoid the slippery slopes* and *casualness causes casualties*. But we take no notice because we do not connect the event to the outcome based on the huge gap between the two. You know that flirting leads to infidelity. You know that lack of maintenance will cause your car's engine to fail. But who cares? Let's put it off or not do it at all.

Your mind is endlessly hungry and curious. It wants to be nurtured and fed. A mind that is given the opportunity to grow and have positive use will enhance your life. Reading regularly, listening to good messages, learning new skills and mastering puzzles can even encourage a positive outcome.

Missing a meal is one thing, but to miss feeding your magnificent brain is neglect of the highest order. Your capacity for learning is almost unlimited. Your highly tuned sports car just needs you to drive it. So it is with your brain.

The idea of time travel strongly exists in our minds. Have you ever wished you could go back to a certain point in your life and do things differently? The outcome would be extraordinary. One small change could alter our lives so much that our current future would be unrecognisable.

We all wish we could go back and change things, but thankfully that's not possible. If we could, the changes that would ensue would be massive. It's because we can't that we should ensure we take greater notice of what's happening in our lives and the choices we are making NOW.

If I could go back to when I was twelve I would tell myself to leave the sweets alone, brush and floss my teeth three times a day and avoid a certain girlfriend who ended up getting me beaten up! That alone would be worth the trip. But if I could live my life over from that point on, knowing what I know now, my life would be so different and to such a point that it would cause chaos to myself and possibly make me very unhappy. That's why the **now** is so important. That's why today is your greatest gift. The present. Realising and grasping that fact can make you powerful, decisive, healthy, rich and wise.

Looking forward, if you met yourself 20 years from now, what would you be saying to yourself? What advice would you give?

What would you tell yourself to change about what you're doing now? There is the answer. You *know* what you'd say. You know and yet you just don't act upon it. Why? Because it's easy not to. Because it is *always* easier to take the line of least resistance and follow the herd.

So if you want to take control of your life you need to focus on the **now**. Each moment of the now determines the future, so plan it. Make use of it as if it were your last breath of oxygen under water. Any seemingly insignificant event can cause a chain reaction over time that massively impacts on your life. It's our choices that make the outcome. Be careful of what you choose. They make or break you. By adopting the smallest of good, healthy habits, you can enhance so much of your life.

Weight training can avoid atrophy. As we get older we naturally lose muscle mass. Just by having a routine of simple weight training we can virtually negate this. Use it or lose it.

A positive effect of looking after your health is you get to spend more time with your children, grandchildren and even beyond. You will be able to enjoy your retirement so much more. Travel becomes easier, as does your mobility.

So, health issues are an accumulation issue. The better your health, the easier it is to handle the tough stuff coming your way. The better an example you are to your loved ones, the easier it is to take advantage of the opportunities that come your way. The more productive you can be, the happier you will be. It all starts with the chocolate bar or eating an apple instead. The gym or the beer? Take your health seriously AND have some fun, but do not let the fun become the only habit.

Being practical

1. Find out your ideal weight, resting heart rate, BMI, cholesterol levels and any other health measurements that may be useful to you. Refer to them often - at least once every six months or more frequently if you can - and remind yourself of your need to keep them near to the ideal.

2. Try to be more aware of the influence that other people have on your health. Do they support or sabotage your health? Increase the former, reduce the latter.

3. Use a personal trainer or coach once a year to design a programme of how to build and maintain good health.

CHAPTER 2

Education

What does an education actually give you? Firstly it shows that you have worked hard, so it suggests you are self-disciplined. Next it shows that, within a given time frame, you are able to reach a certain standard. It also helps to compare you to others. All this sounds great... and it is. Acquiring knowledge, understanding and wisdom makes you more valuable to the marketplace that you are learning in.

Learn to be a brain surgeon and you will eventually be paid £1,000 an hour for your skills. Learn to read literature and interpret Shakespeare and you can become valuable in a different arena, which might not pay as much but could be invaluable in many other ways. Shakespeare was a great story teller and his ideas and stories have influenced the lives of millions. Learn how to fix an engine and, using that skill set, you'll get the going rate as a mechanic.

What you learn is one thing...

How you learn to apply it is another.

Fixing an engine is an hourly rate employed skill. Running a business is not. That same mechanic could also use his time learning how to build a business and make it profitable. He could then employ ten mechanics and earn a slice from each. His earnings would not only be unrelated to the actual mechanical work but, whether he is there or not, he will still get paid for work done. If he is on holiday and has set the business up to run without him, he is in a fortunate position which will exceed his original skillset as a mechanic. Take it a step further, and should he wish to continue working as a mechanic he would gain financially on both counts, as an employer and a senior mechanic.

All the wealth that was generated for Ray Croc who founded *McDonald's* franchises was done without him serving a burger. His ideas and the application of them, earned him a fortune. Did he earn whilst on holiday? Yes. Did he earn while he was sleeping at night? Yes. His restaurants are all over the world.

The skills we teach our children serve them for life. Give a man a fish and you'll feed him for a day, teach him to fish and you feed him and his family for life. So, for me, education comes in many forms: formal education, entrepreneurial skills and life skills, are just a few. All have merit and all have their place.

So how do we educate ourselves, our children and friends? Do we go through the formal education route only? Or, do we acquire and use all aspects of life's tools and wisdom? How available is this information? Surprisingly so. It can be found in abundance in libraries, books, programmes, seminars, and podcasts offered by successful and wealthy people who are willing to share their knowledge. And then there are the people around us: colleagues, friends and mentors, who we are in regular contact with. We can acquire knowledge and understanding from the people we choose to spend time with.

Going to church each week will expose you to the Wisdom of Solomon and well-known wise men from history, all sharing their knowledge. If you believe in God then even the words of His son are there in red in the bible for you read. Such wisdom. So easy to learn.

Here again, we come to the gap between what people could do and actually choose to do. It's easy to see how. It's the *negative* accumulated effect of a lack of education. Some people never read a book once they leave school. Do not forget to feed your brain.

How many people have a library ticket? Just three percent. Is it hard to get one? No. So why only three percent? I think it is because it's easier not to. Start to tell everyone that their library is about to close down and you'll get an influx of new members wanting to save it. Start a world war and the churches fill up. Most of us want to obtain wisdom. Please do not await a catastrophe to trigger you wanting to obtain it.

Kids don't lack the ability to learn, they just lack the teachers. They lack the right role models. Without supervision they will get up to all sorts of things. Their minds are searching for leadership and knowledge. Teenage boys often destroy things because they want to take things apart and understand how they work. A class, demonstrating how to take things apart and put them back together, is a positive accumulation of knowledge. Without the right teaching children will find their own way of learning by trial and error. Leave them to their own devises and they may never get the education or life skills that can set them free from what Bob Geldof calls the *Rat Trap.*

Let's decide what we want to learn and gradually fill up our minds with knowledge that truly interest us as well as giving us perspective: formal learning for show or as a requirement for employment and life skills for everything else. The wisdom is out there and, not only is it free, it is easier to obtain than ever before.

Today's internet is yesterday's library. You can search it for anything. Everyone has a virtual library ticket in their hand; one to the largest, easiest-to-search library that has ever existed. Is it seen that way by you?

Being practical

1. Read every day and have a balanced approach about what you read: history, inspirational, practical, cautionary, biographical, as well as novels that contain a lesson. It's nutrition for the brain. Reading low-grade sensationalist fodder is like going through a bin to find a good morsel of food. You'll waste a lot of time and likely be disappointed. So pick the good stuff. Accumulate the wisdom.

2. Get a formal education if you can, in a subject that you love and inspires you. Many people in the world are denied the chance.

3. Listen to those that have been there and done it. Seek them out. The insights and guidance you can get from them is

invaluable. Many people too are generous with their wisdom and knowledge. They're keen to teach you because they do not want you to make the same mistakes they did. It is a compliment to be asked to share your wisdom. Enjoy paying compliments. Feel free to share your knowledge with those that seek it. This serves you too.

CHAPTER 

Money

Okay, so money is important. That multi-coloured piece of paper in your pocket that is so difficult to forge is money but people lose sight of what it really is. It's exchanged for goods or services and can be exchanged again and again, giving multiple choices for its use. It can also give massive freedom and set others free. It can reduce suffering, be wasted, burnt, saved, invested and a whole host of other things too. It can make you happy if you let it. It can also make you unhappy too. It has a way of being accumulated like anything else but, like oxygen, you'll know very quickly when you don't have any.

The choices you make now affect its future availability to you. What you do today could make it scarcer in the future. But what you do today could equally make it abundant. Not every decision or choice you make works out the way you'd hope. Too much money just makes you more of what you already are; if you are a generous person, it is likely you will be more generous. If you are mean, money has a way of magnifying that character trait too.

When I talk about money, it is never about the crinkly pieces of paper or the numbers on a bank statement. It is about the freedom, the power and the wonder of the ability to have something that transcends all borders and religions and languages and bias. In our modern world, it is the ability to be free from slavery or help your fellow man, all of which can be achieved by the accumulation of wealth.

I am from an age when I remember my own father working both a full-time job in a factory and a bar job in the evenings to make ends meet. Despite his advanced skills as a toolmaker, his full-time wages were not enough to meet his family's basic needs. While my sister, brother and I were at school, my mother worked part-time in order to earn extra money so we could have the extra treats such as a week or two holiday each year. I even remember my mum and dad buying me a calculator costing £12.99 when I was 12 years old. It was one of those with red number displays. That was a lot of money then. I loved that calculator. I have no idea what happened to it in the end but it changed the way I thought about the future. Again, this is another example of an accumulative effect. I saw a different future based on one item.

You see, being broke is tough to handle. It does motivate in many ways but often not for the good. When you can feel the benefits of being financially secure, you get to achieve more, experience more and gather more. Remember to develop your money tree.

Maslow's Hierarchy of Needs explains where your priorities instinctively lie:

1. Food and shelter
2. Security and safety
3. Achievement and esteem

Once you master the basic needs you can relax and enjoy life more easily. That motivates you to want more or to ensure what you have achieved is safe. Money itself is not intrinsically evil, but it's the heart, the essence behind its use and gathering that determines its power and validity, good or bad.

We all get mixed up in many ways over almost everything but money is something you can count, allocate, account for, give, reduce fear with, bring joy with, see things you would never otherwise have been able to and above all bring safety and security. It can also bring massive pleasure. How you read this sentence will determine your heart. That in turn will determine your outcomes, drive and joy from it. It is never about the money. Money is just the tool by which we can measure what we can do. Greed is not good.

Getting knock backs is par for any course. Given the nature of money and people's thirst for it, you are in for some tricky times when trying to accumulate any decent sizeable amounts of it. A fool and his money are easily parted as the saying goes; it burns a hole in their pocket.

Take lottery winners for example. It is not a surprise that so few genuinely have the character to handle it. When my wife and I talk about winning ten million pounds, it takes ten minutes of deciding what to do with it before the cracks of disagreement begin to show themselves. It is like getting to the top floor too quickly. You will get dizzy and will hanker to get down again. You have to take the stairs and acclimatise. Zig Ziglar's book *'See You at The Top'*, talks about the journey and the eventual acceptance of all that you need to do to be able to handle wealth and status comfortably.

Zig Ziglar is in his nineties and has been a motivational speaker for most of his life. His programmes and books sell all over the world. I consider the man to be a genius. So for me his accumulated wisdom is real treasure. This is an example of who to study the teachings of.

Being successful in not about money. It is about what you become when you pursue success. Money is a measure of success but definitely not the only one. Your opinion of your money is better for you, if it was deserved rather than at the cost of others. That's why I think the accumulation of effort and time are the best teachers of not only how to handle money, but how to enjoy it and use it for good.

Some of us are lucky enough to live in a society today where we can do almost anything we want. We can be on the other side of the world in less than 24 hours, let alone around the world in 80 days! What makes life so wonderful is the opportunity to do as we wish with it. Yes we can screw it up easily. Yes we can get a curve ball thrown at us on too regular a basis. But how we handle it is still down to us.

Many people in the world, do not have this type of freedom and for those who do, I believe we have a duty to share that fought for freedom and bring joy to as many corners of the world that we can. I do not wish to impose my beliefs, I mean to help people be free of tyranny, persecution, dictators and harsh regimes that stop people being happy and safe. I hope to allow them to have a basic education or even a good one. To allow medical help be given to those who truly need it. That should be our goal as humans. To be able to do this and sustain the planet without damaging it, would be wonderful. Money can help us work towards that. Our freedom came about from the accumulation of decisions by our forefathers. Some paid with their lives to give us the freedom we have today.

I remember the feeling of being heartbroken over not having enough money to buy something of importance. That *only-buy-what's-needed* feeling. That *if-only-I-had-enough-to-buy-that* feeling. We are surrounded by wealth in this world yet 70 percent are still poor. Is it because we keep making the wrong choices being too common? Well in some cases yes. Is it because some people live in a society that makes the wrong choices for them? Well in some cases yes also. Is it because we are lazy, lack the drive or courage? Again sometimes yes. But overall it is not because the opportunities are not around us. It is easier for me to say this in a country of freedom and opportunities. Yet Japan, after the Second World War was amongst the poorest in the world. As a country they chose to prosper, and within 30 years, became one of the wealthiest nations on earth. With no natural resources other than its people, they decided to use the opportunities they had.

It takes guts and determination to achieve things. It sometimes takes so much motivation that it feels like it will break our spirit.

However, one thing is for sure, the capacity humans have is enormous. Money brings out the basic instincts for survival separate from the street fight or defending yourself from being beaten. Money brings out the desire to have more food on the table than you need to eat. Money can make you betray a friend or cheat a loved one.

It is with great emotion that I desire to bring out the right motivation with a follow through plan to make the honest person in you shine with confidence and pride in knowing that you not only achieved great things, you eased the burden of others along the way and left a legacy that will help others do the same. Not an overweight lonely person who got great wealth but with no one left to love within their life. "You can't buy memories" as a good friend said to me once.

What makes money accumulate? Property, saving, generating income from your skills, creating a business that makes money whether you work in it or not, winning it, gambling, stealing, being given it or even finding it.

Let's rule out the ones that just don't really help in practical terms. Gambling is mostly a mug's game, stealing is always a mug's game, finding it is just very unlikely and being given it will be lucky but not help you if you do not know how to handle it. So looking at the ways you can accumulate money, let's cover one of the big ones.

Property

If you bought a three bedroom semi-detached house in central England in 1975 it would have cost you about £3,500. In 2005 that same property would be worth £175,000. That's 5,000 percent growth over 30 years.

Is that a good deal? Well £3,500 invested in a bank account with an average deposit return of say seven percent would have achieved £26,642.88. A mere 15 percent of the same result with a house. However, along the way if you factor in mortgage payments, maintenance costs, insurance costs, heating costs, and so on, as well as the benefit of having somewhere to live all that time. The advantages and disadvantages of what's a good investment get very blurred.

Now if you had bought two houses and rented one out that covered all those extra costs, it gets easier to see why it was a good thing to do. However, this raises issues such as taxation. When you do finally realise that asset into cash, the government wants its share in the form of capital gains tax. This can be a huge dent in your profits. However, again if you had ten houses, you may not give a fig that you made nearly two million pounds and then had to pay £700,000 of it in tax. So therein lies the dilemma with property. Can it make money over the long-term? Well usually yes. Can it be a pain in the neck over that time? Well usually yes too. Tenants are not always as polite and cooperative as all landlords would like them to be. They don't always pay on time and there could be down sides such as them not paying you at all or when you have too many properties for rent but no tenants for a while. Property is a difficult asset to convert to ready cash. This makes its value unstable, so a long-term view is needed.

I do believe however, that property is a must in any portfolio of investment. It does need to be given a very hard look in the eye though. Get too emotive about it and it can cause you big worries. Get very factual and practical about it and it can be a blessing.

A large proportion of the money made on property is made during the first six months. You just have to buy at the right price. Sounds easy, but isn't. Going to see 50 properties before buying your first one is not a discipline that most investors would be willing to do. It is the best thing you could do though. Only then will you know your market place. Only then will you know what makes the difference between a distressed seller and a smart estate agent getting you to buy at full market price. Not being the type to haggle and walk away when the dealing gets tough will hinder your accumulation of wealth for years. A poor decision can cost you five to ten years of not having £500,000 for instance. That's a big cost but if you look at the decisions you make today and roll them forward by 30 years, it is amazing how much is affected by so little.

Let's take an example. Each time you go to the petrol station, whilst in the queue you decide to buy a chocolate bar for, say, 60 pence. You do this three times a week. £1.80 a week is not a lot now, but the accumulated effects are huge. One, your body weight may increase by about three pounds a year on that basis. That's 90 pounds in weight over a 30 year period. Your savings will be lighter by about £2,808, but not just that, the interest you would have earned on it could easily be as much as £15,000.

Now assume that during that time you had used say £3000 of that money to buy a house in 1970, at 5000% growth it would have been £150,000. Now that could be used today to buy ten houses with £15,000 deposit on each and then the money would be building at a nice rate. I know this is an exaggeration but it isn't that far from the truth is it? What slips through our fingers on a daily basis is enough to make us wealthy in its own right. Cigarettes are the classic one and one I use often as an example. They are around £8.00 a packet now and some people buy one packet a day. The cost in monetary terms alone is ridiculous.

Being practical

1. When you consider money as a tool for good it becomes easier to plan for, accumulate and build with. Give it the respect it deserves. Save, invest and be charitable. *The Richest Man in Babylon* by Richard Clayson suggests ten percent of your net earnings be used for these three. Learn to live on the rest.

2. Live well within your earnings, and save before you spend. Decide on what you want to save each month and put that away first. Then only spend what you have left over. Learn how to be more valuable to the marketplace and this will increase your earnings.

3. Seek professional advice for investing or learn how to do it properly. Taking care to be ethical and respectful will enhance your respect for wealth. Using the knowledge of running your own business, reducing your taxation and building income that generates for you, even if you are not working for it, can all be learnt from professionals who advise on financial matters.

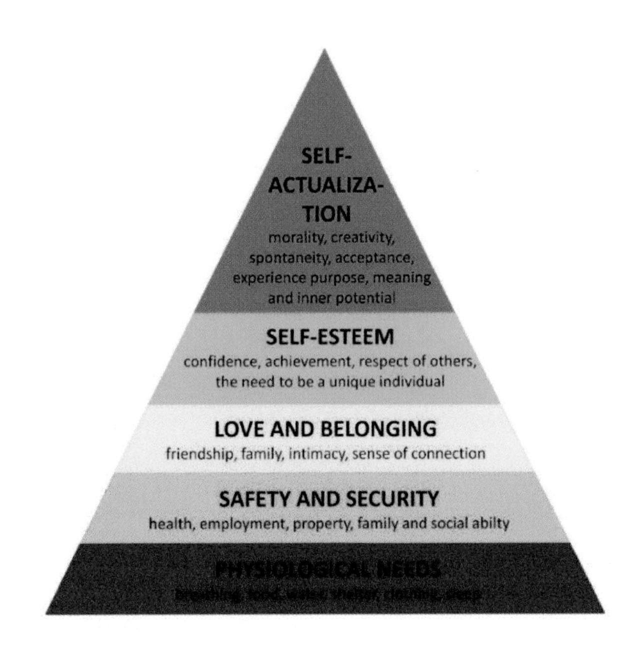

Maslow's Hierarchy of Needs

There are many versions of this table and although quite self-explanatory the subject is worthy of study. Your motivation is triggered by many events and understanding your own motivation and transitions that life gives you.

CHAPTER 4

Relationships

How do you treat your friends? Are they disposable? Convenient? Valued? Rare? Are they treasured or a pain in the neck? What do you do for and with them that makes a difference in their lives?

No one is an island. It is not in our nature to be alone, so trust and care of others is a necessary glue which hold us together. Relationships may be more valuable than anything else we ever have.

If you treat relationships too casually you know you'll end up lonely and sad. They are so valuable that it is hard to explain the hurt you feel when a loved one becomes an enemy or when a good friend becomes someone who hates you and will try to ridicule you at every turn. Worse still when a child becomes so disconnected from you that the relationship cannot be recovered. A nurtured relationship on the other hand is a joy to celebrate and be thankful for.

A thoughtful card or flowers can make a relationship healthier. The sacrifice of time can build a rapport that endures. What is it that you do today that helps keep these irreplaceable intangibles alive and healthy? So please consider the accumulation of what you currently do. Will it nurture the relationship? Someone said to me once, 'How do children spell love?' T.I.M.E. was the answer. Are you spending enough time with those you love and want in your future?

We all experience betrayal at some time in our lives. We all go through the destruction that it causes when we have made too many wrong decisions and not enough of the right ones. Keep the ongoing effects of your interaction in your mind at all times.

The cheating husband eventually tears himself apart with guilt and lack of peace of mind. He's a liar and a user who, when found out or admits to his infidelity, destroys all that was good around him. If he's lucky he may be forgiven, but the relationship will never be the same again and the hurt he causes lasts a lifetime. The strength of a great marriage is nurtured by the woven experiences and respect that comes from giving it the attention it deserves, accumulated over time.

The smallest decision, leads to another. Making or taking the wrong path may not seem important or even significant at the time but, over years, the consequences of such a choice can become huge. In the film *Vanilla Sky*, Tom Cruise talks about,

"The little things, there is nothing bigger."

One decision leads to another and this becomes a habit or trap and before you are aware, it can become damaged or too late to recover; you find yourself immersed in an irreconcilable situation. Or, you can weave a strong thread that becomes a strong rope and is a delightful strength.

I'm reminded of the story of the frog who, accidently jumped into a saucepan and, in the tepid water was feeling comfortable, sleepy and relaxed. He didn't notice the heat had been turned on until it was too late. He couldn't get out and ended up boiled through complacency.

We need significant others in our lives and we need to protect the relationships we have and any mistake should be stamped on immediately. Learn from the frog story. Don't just dismiss it as a little story. Really learn from it.

Making a conscious effort to be connected, complimentary, kind and helpful, rarely goes unnoticed. It is so rewarding to have trust with friends and family in a way that is strong and reliable.

The accumulation of neglect, complacency and detachment will undermine the strongest of bonds. The opposite is true too though. Respect for, caring, and involvement build a deep connection. When things do go wrong, it is easier to heal and repair. When you consider the relationships in your life, try to imagine the strength of them as a bank account. The more you put in the stronger it gets.

Being Practical

1. Send a hand written letter to those distant people you care about. It is much better than an email, or a Facebook comment. Electronic attention is better than none, but writing is very powerful. Ideally, call them as well. Skype is a wonderful tool for this.

2. Listen more than you speak. Two ears and one mouth signify the amount we should use them.

"Seek first to understand and then be understood."

as Stephen R. Covey suggests in his book *Seven Habits of Highly Effective People.* Listen with the intent to understand rather than to reply.

3. Keep your word or promises. If you think you cannot do so, tell them. Your integrity is what makes a relationship strong. The time you spend with them is important but so is keeping your word. Cancelling meeting up with a terrific friend to then be able to meet up with a casual acquaintance may seem okay with you, but please do not let it become the norm.

4. Draw a circle and place the names of the most important relationships in your life. These should always come first for attention and connection. Decisions involving them should have a consideration in relation to the impact on them first.

"If I meditate 30
minutes each day
I feel terrific,
fantastic even.
If I am too
busy to meditate,
then I need to do an
hour each day."

Jack Black

CHAPTER 5

Your Spiritual Belief

I have a belief in God and that faith has steered me at times when I know I would have set the wrong wheels in motion or taken a wrong turn had I not had it. I do not know how or when or why my faith emerged but I do know that I am a better person with it than I would have been without it.

Many people I know are surprised when they learn about my depth of faith because I can swear like the rest of them, get drunk and I'm even not very Christian-like at times.

My martial art hobby helps me deal with my aggressive tendencies. My scuba diving helps me relax bringing a calm I would describe as spiritual. I love riding my motorcycle and that focus and delight of amazing technology with its comforts, speed and skill need, takes me to an inner place, it is hard to comprehend. I can only call it spiritual because all of these things give me a feeling that there is a spiritual realm that helps us all. Some call it God, Christianity and many other faith names. For me it is who we are inside; I feel steered by a greater power than I can understand. So much of how we feel is, of course, experiential. However, when you find harmony and wonder in things that you can't describe with words; that to me is a spiritual experience, like a glow of pride or a feeling of great love.

Here's the rub. When you face events that seem to be overwhelming you will likely find your god. I often ask for divine help and when I have, I have found answers to my prayers.

My advice is this. If you have any faith in the spiritual realms then you should explore it. They are usually positive and will provide a moral compass. Without a doubt, all of us think in spiritual terms at some point in our lives; when someone we know dies or falls seriously ill, when we get threatened or when we just wish for better things.

Those quiet moments when nothing but our own thoughts are there, it's quite encouraging to find that even talking to yourself can seem like a spiritual event. Do not ignore doing this.

Many times we can find ways to lift ourselves through self-talk. But sometimes it is not talk, it's a feeling or an awareness that takes us to a deeper level. That inspirational thought or idea that comes from seemingly nowhere.

There is such wealth in exploring our inner self. When have you thought of someone and found them calling you not long after? When have you wished for something in earnest and it happens? Is this a coincidence? I think not. If it is, then that's amazing. If it isn't and you're ignoring it, you are missing out. There is great strength to be gained from practicing tuning into your spiritual self.

Meditation helps here tremendously. If you've never tried it then you are in for a treat when you do. It calms the nerves, lowers your blood pressure, aids sleeping and most of all it often provides you with a huge raft of new ideas. You'll wonder how you existed without it.

Quiet contemplative reflection tunes you into your subconscious mind's ideas and creativity. Just imagine an ideas box that you can visit anytime and draw on that can improve everything you do. The box is there at your disposal and is larger than you can comprehend. Go to it. You can use these ideas for the rest of your life, without charge or guilt because they are yours. Imagine having a Ferrari on your drive and the keys in your pocket and its log book says it is yours but you are just not bothering to even use it! That's what ignoring your imagination and your spiritual side is like.

The first time I tried deep meditation, I was taken aback. Clear and concise ideas and images came flooding through. It is hard to find the time to do it properly as you need to be quiet and relaxed. It does take practice and discipline.

Jack Black, one of the greats in this field, considers it so necessary that to not be able to meditate is an unhealthy state to find yourself in.

Make the time and stress falls away. Ideas that will help you and your peace of mind will flow and develop with practice. Yes, meditation needs practice but so does anything worthwhile.

The accumulation of the use of this skill is very beneficial. The accumulation effect of not doing it is neglect of yourself. The medical world recognises that it is beneficial too.

Transcendental Meditation groups have been tested by the medical professions and there are published papers on the benefits of practiced meditation in *The Lancet*. Check out http://uk.tm.org/health-benefits for the list of benefits. There are many forms, apps and classes these days. Seek out your own style and preference.

I am re-reading this draft after years of the original writing and this has reminded me of why I should always be doing it. We need down-time other than just sleep. Keep this as being as important in your life as eating or exercising.

A friend gave me an idea of how magnificent the brain we have works. Imagine you have some seeds to give to some birds that are in the park. If you see them on the grass and run at them to give them the seed, they will scatter and fly away. If you approach calmly and put a little seed down they will come to you. If you stay calm, more will come and before you know it you will have an abundance of birds. So it is with our thoughts and ideas and our spiritual self. We need to approach our creativity and problem solving from a calm nurturing stance that allows the wonders of its ability to show itself.

Spiritually we are, in my view, linked and dependent on each other in more ways than we may care to realise. At least if you get in touch with your spiritual side no matter how you do it, you will get a chance to make up your own mind. That's always the best place to start. Where that leads you will be unique and therapeutic. So please do not ignore it. It is not about finding God, it is about discovering your inner depths and your own version of spirituality. It is there, you just have to be quiet enough to listen to it.

Being Practical

1. Learn to find time to discover, process and accumulate the thoughts that are in your own subconscious. Without a quiet place for them to come to the surface, they are lost or unheard in this noisy, busy life that's full of distractions.

2. Reflect on what the word 'Spiritual' means to you. Write it down, meditate on it and explore your ideas about what it is to you.

3. If you feel stressed, it is often because you are not taking enough time, to healthily reflect and process why you could be stressed. Give yourself a score of one to ten during different times of the day, to allow you to identify

what, and to what level, causes you stress. Recognise too what calms you and to what level. Take time out to reflect on both extremes to give your subconscious a chance to reduce the negative effect.

CHAPTER 6

Your Peace of Mind

As we get older we value our peace of mind more and more. Age and experience may have taught us through hard lessons so we know its worth. It seems when we are young we are easily troubled but things get solved relatively simply in comparison to when we are older. There seems to be more complexity to our problems and hence our peace becomes more and more disturbed. Take friends for instance: as a school kid we fell out and made up easily. My daughter relates to a friend who has been a friend and a non-friend a dozen times. But when we are older, a bust up with a friend can be very traumatic and seemingly unrecoverable.

As we get older, things trouble us that cause us to lose our equilibrium: a row with a neighbour that stops us ever talking to each other, a business partnership gone sour that just seems to affect every area of our lives. Another example is a relationship or marriage break-up and the feeling of being out of kilter can become overwhelming.

A good solution to all this is to understand what it is that in your view is right and what isn't. Is it right that you fell out over a misunderstanding? Was it worth losing your peace of mind to stick to your guns? Would forgiving the person make life easier for you? It is obvious and hard to relate to, but to not forgive hurts you more than it hurts anyone else.

When you can put your head on the pillow at night and find that you just fall into a deep sleep and have good dreams, the chances are you have a clear conscience and peace of mind.

Now admittedly we all have different levels of conscience. Some people see stealing from an insurance company as just fair game. For instance, do you know anyone who has cheated on a contents insurance claim and felt no twinge of conscience whatsoever?

The important stance to take is this; how would I feel had I been the one swindled? If you are okay with that then your conscience is likely to be clear. But true inner peace comes from being better than that.

You would like help in an unfortunate situation but would not expect it. If you go out of your way to help others who don't expect it, then you find an inner peace that lifts you to a higher level. However, there is a twinge of selfishness here in that you find yourself justifying what you've done to make yourself feel better and it becomes an act for you *and* the recipient. In my opinion the true way to help others and get good lasting peace of mind from it is to anonymously help someone or do something for the benefit of others. This gives you no glory at all and it becomes a wonderful feeling of peace, knowing that it has been done for the purest of reasons. It works for me so why not try it and make your own decision.

A voucher for food offered to a homeless person is better than money. If you can give it to them and walk away before they see what it is, it will have a great impact. There is nothing wrong of course with just giving it face to face. It is a personal thing for sure, but I personally like to give and help, without the recipient knowing from where it came. I feel better then. The random acts of kindness idea was extended in a wonderful film called *'Pay it Forward'*. I suggest watching it to help you be touched by its ideas.

Another example is of the boy who was asked to give a blood transfusion for his sister who was dying of leukaemia. The boy agreed knowing it would save his sister. But secretly later he took the doctor aside and asked, *'When will I start to die? After I have given my blood to her or later?'* You see the boy selflessly agreed thinking he would die in the process. I'm using this as an example to show that kindness can be huge and beneficial as well as small. It does give you a great sense of wellbeing which leads to peace.

Peace comes in all guises. One is in terms of money. When you think of all the money you have let slip through your fingers each year of your life you can start to wince. But saving stops that from becoming a concern and an upset to your harmony.

When you consider that your accumulated study has led you to the point of understanding that you have now, it unnerves you to realise that there was so much more you could have done. And were that to be the case, chances are your income, lifestyle or social standing would be better than it is now. Your relationship could have benefitted more from a greater level of knowledge too.

What peace of mind have we given up by not seizing the day? How many of us would like to get extra time back with a departed loved one, or be able to go back to a younger time and start again?

If we prepare by taking advantage of as much as we can that is available it will always help our peace of mind. The balanced life that many of us seek is available in bite-size pieces only. We cannot get it overnight or by studying Buddhism for a week. It can only be obtained by accumulated effort.

Peace comes from relaxation, feeling safe, learning what is right, being trustworthy, feeling loved and loving as well as a hundred other things. What we need to ask ourselves is this: what am I doing today to improve that peace of mind? Could what I am doing today jeopardise it either immediately or long-term? If the answer to either is not what you want to hear, then please rethink. It is better to change course now rather than later.

We all make unwise decisions. We are all foolhardy and make silly mistakes, as we are not perfect, just human. However, we do have the power of choice. That power defines our future and can make it a blessing or a curse.

I know, I have made some bad choices myself. I have sacrificed too much for making a cowardly or poor decision. Let me tell you here and now, attempting to avoid short-term angst ultimately results in long-term pain. It isn't worth the long-term pain, to avoid the short-term pain. Sometimes doing the right thing comes at what *feels* like an initial heavy price, but long-term it does help to make the harder choices quickly. I postponed selling a property once. The value dropped and I lost quite a bit of money. My only reason for delay was I knew it would cause frustrations with the co-owner. It was right for both of us that we sold it as quickly as possible but she didn't feel she could easily cope with the upheaval. So I left it for a while. The cost in the delay was enormous; she still had the upheaval just at a later date, and this was compounded by the significant loss of money. I should have been stronger. I wimped out really.

Doing the right thing is often harder than doing something that will allow you to temporarily forget it. Peace of mind comes from doing the right thing even when it is the hardest.

Peace of mind comes from avoiding things too. The temptation to get involved in something that you should not, or that you know is unworthy, can be a decision that gets you much criticism. Crowd or group peer pressure can be awfully strong. It is at times like this that you need your resolve to be solid, if knowing the long-term effects could be disastrous. It helps if you think of the accumulation effect and the potential for undermining your peace of mind. It is this style of thinking that can be your guide and strength when faced with these dilemmas.

Being Practical

1. Start a review of your moral compass. What things are okay and what are not, to you? Discuss them with a trusted friend, partner or loved one. Gauging your own acceptance levels rather than what you think others consider acceptable, is key to gaining peace of mind. Decide to do what is right quickly.

2. Set yourself goals. Remember we are at peace by 'being' and 'doing'. We are not just human beings, we are human doings too. A sense of achievement brings high levels of peace of mind. By setting goals and focusing on the progress towards them rather than the shortfall, we create calm and peace based on a sense of worth.

3. Forgive those who have wronged you. Whether or not you tell them that you forgive them is not always

an easy decision, so firstly forgive them in your thoughts, let that sink in, and be guided by how you feel about it. If you then want to take the next step and it feels right for you, and it safe to do so, then follow that thought and tell them. If it isn't, then don't.

"Start by doing what is
NECESSARY,

then do what is
POSSIBLE,

and suddenly you will find
yourself doing the
IMPOSSIBLE."

Francis of Assisi

CHAPTER 7

Time

Money can give you freedom like nothing else can. We all know that those with loads of time on their hands and limited money are usually the unemployed, the state benefit reliant or those who are retired on a small pension.

People with lots of money and no time on their hands are usually management, directors or CEOs. Those with little money and no time are often the lowly paid poor skill level employed. Those with abundant time and money are the people with cash or assets that produce cash. They may or may not choose to get involved in the assets' management. They can choose what to do with their time or have earned enough, retired and made good use of their money to be comfortable.

Now when you consider the options, you can choose to be in one or the other of these categories by applying a few basic disciplines.

We all only have 24 hours per day, unless we die that day. We never know really when our number is up and no one gets to buy extra time above anyone else. So time is a precious commodity; an irreplaceable luxury that should be given the respect that it deserves. Unless you want to spend all your time making money and none enjoying it then you have to plan and use time as efficiently as possible. Doing so will help you become more balanced, happier, fulfilled and - importantly - avoid regret. Use all 24 hours to the best of your ability.

What really then is a good use of time? Well here are a few tricks that do help. One, if you have a big job to do then break it down into small pieces and attack it a piece at a time. If you have a small job to do, then estimate how long it will take you and then use the next slot of that time period up doing it. I often have a 'to do' list with small jobs to do that just need to be done but will only take five or ten minutes such as needing to repair a drawer or tidy an area. If I find myself between bigger things I want to get done and have ten minutes to spare, I look at my 'To-Dos' and pick one I can finish in that time. If I have estimated what time it will take to do it, I can pick it knowing I have time and just get on with it.

I often find myself with 15 minutes spare before an appointment. So I use that time to write a letter or polish my shoes or make a quick phone call and so on. This makes sure I don't waste time.

Many people use To-Do lists and I must say they are a big help. However, the best way I have found to use time is to prioritise. Think about what needs to be done first and attack that as much as possible and then move on to what needs to be done next. This can be misleading though. For instance, I need plenty of time to prepare for up and coming meetings or presentations. So, I see that preparation as important and urgent because if I start to get short of time for that job then I get it wrong and start to get very stressed about it, less productive and time is lost. Things that are both non-urgent and non-important get put to the bottom of my list and are attacked last or not at all.

Let's consider money. What needs to be done timely about money? Well one instance is that if we leave saving for retirement till later it can easily become too late. Yet, attack it early and it gets easier and less stressful. The first pound invested makes the most money.

If you want to invest in the stock market then timing is highly important but it may not be today. Shares in Lloyds used to fluctuate in a band width that was fairly predictable: between £4 and £6. I used to buy at £4, wait until they reached £6 and sell them. Then when they dropped to £4 again I would use the initial amount and the profit and buy some more. It is not as easy as it sounds but this is an illustration of timing.

Personally I like to save regularly whether I feel I need to or not, regardless of what the savings account balance is because experience has proven to me that I will need this money at some point even if I can't see why now. Accumulation of money happens best over time as well as what it is used for. For instance, property over long periods will likely rise in value as well. So timing and the type of investment are linked.

Time plays a factor in many things. The army talk about the best time for sleep. In any 24 hour period there is a time when your body needs sleep. However, it is not as much as you think. You can get by on only four hours if you know exactly when your body needs them. Even less with training. Your sleep need is like your finger print. It is unique. The right sleep at the right time is very rejuvenating. Lying in bed all day may be the worst way to recharge your batteries.

Knowing when is the best time for you to sleep gives you more energy for the time you are awake. If that also gives you more time awake then you have more time to be more productive and proactive. More time to do more of the things you like and the things you should do or need to do. You will also do them more effectively. My best time for writing is between 10.00pm and 1.00 am. My best time for sleep is between 2.00 am and 9.00 am and between 3.00 pm and 5.00pm. If I sleep at least six of those hours in a 24 hour period then I am happy, strong and alert. If I try to sleep at other times, it is dream laden or broken sleep and I wake up more tired than when I went to bed. Just by managing your sleep better you can gain significant amounts of time. One hour a day for 40 years accumulates to 600 extra days.

It isn't always possible to make the best use of our time. It is possible however to try to do so. That's what gives you an edge. Those people who seem to get to bed at 9.30pm and wake up at 5.30am wide awake do so because they can get the best sleep for them at a time when it least disturbs anyone else. I seem to be always battling to get the right hours because my world is not built around my best hours.

Time obviously gets more precious as you get older. Many older people make better use of time for two reasons. One, their experience allows them to know how to and two, they become more and more aware of the limitation of their time. Awareness, value of time and wisdom create a wonderful mix of the efficient and mature use of time. Only the young think life is long.

'Youth is wasted on the young' it is said. Opportunities are also wasted on the stupid. So many opportunities come your way and, unless you are prepared, they slip through your fingers. 'Luck favours the prepared, darling' as Edna says in the Pixar film *'The Incredibles.'* Be ready and plan the use of your time.

It is easy to say this but one day you will face the reality of 'Oh damn! I wish I had done this or done that when I could have, rather than keep putting it off'. It is inevitable that we all will run out of time.

Facing our own demise is challenging. I have had the opportunity to meet with two people who had only a few days to live due to cancer and have asked them the question, what do you recommend a younger man like me should do with his life? The two answers were very similar. Firstly they both said, 'I would worry less if I had my time over again.' Secondly they both said they wish they had used their time more effectively and given more of it to those they love. Other issues were to not get upset over trivial things and also to just be happier. I heard that happiness is based on an accumulation of good memories rather than things. Could have, should have and didn't, will lead to regret. If only, is the common phrase we are used to. In the superb film *'Meet Joe Black',* the lead character played by Anthony Hopkins is facing his death. Talking to his daughter he says that he has lived his life, without regrets. It is wonderful to have done so. Seize the time you have at your disposal, so that you can say the same. Don't be the one always saying, "I'll get around to it."

A poor sense of time is what keeps us off guard. Years seem like decades until they are done. New Year's Day always seems cold to me in a way that it reminds me that another year has slipped by which may not have been as fulfilled as much as I would have liked. Setting goals and writing a journal helps to slow things down. Taking pictures along the way and taking the time out to savour the air and flowers is the other way to slow things down but by far the best is to take time to reflect. Set aside time to contemplate: an hour for the week, a day for the year and so on. It helps to avoid the feeling of regret.

This reflective time does have a great effect. It does put things in their place and help make them last longer. A friend once said to me that if you make now a good time then every time you look back on it you get to enjoy it again. Looking back over bad stuff just reinforces the bad stuff. So make now good. Use New Year's Day to reflect on what you achieved in the last twelve months and use the emotion to set some goals for the next year.

Again this is an example of the accumulative effect. It is your choice. Make the right choices in a timely fashion and then it all adds up to a great sum. Watching others who have done so, when you haven't is a truly disheartening experience.

It is the accumulation and combination of time, money and values that construct the framework of our lives and have led you to the outcome you are experiencing now.

Explore the sides of how these interact. Be aware of how these three impact each other in your life. Sacrificing too much time to obtain money is out of balance for your use of time. Compromising your values to obtain money is a poor use of your choices. Being kind, truthful and treating money with respect but not worshipping it will create an outcome you can feel at peace with.

The future test. Helping you make better decisions.

When it comes to anything in your life there is always a decision to be made. Even if it is no decision, that's a decision not to do something or to do nothing. So the first part is to make sure that you have a decision process in place.

Most decisions can be made very quickly and if you are the type that's used to doing so, it is rare for it to be an issue. We are not all like this of course, and that's what makes us unique. So what do I mean by the future test?

A good rule of thumb is of course to practice making better decisions. Rather than go into a decision tree scenario, which are rigid formulae that keep you on track but lack the use of intuition and imagination. I often see them in financial advice programmes. A flowchart is a poor system for decisions, in my opinion I would follow what I call the future test.

We are all used to making decisions about the here and now; we list the pros and cons, or talk with peers and friends and the guy down the pub and so on. However, most of us don't look at the direction the decision will take us. If you were flying across the Atlantic and were only one degree out at the start, you could end up 200 miles away from your original desired destination. Obvious, yes, but most of us tend to get started on something and agree with ourselves to adjust along the way, just as a plane would for instance, unaware that it is veering way off course.

The future test is not only more helpful with the decision making process, but gets you off to a better start and more importantly will give you a deeper understanding of what it is about the decision that really matters.

Let's suppose you decide to join a gym and get fitter. Good decision, albeit incomplete due to not being defined. If we get more specific about what we want to achieve we can apply the future test. 'Get fitter' could mean lose some excess body fat. It could mean have a resting heart rate of below 60, have a BMI of 20 percent and be able to run a marathon in a specific time.

So, firstly, why am I joining? Next, when am I going to actually go? Then what am I going to do? After that comes the best bit: what would be the long-term effect of me doing this? Will I feel better, will I look better, be sexier, have a happier life and so on?

The future reflection of your decisions will make them better ones and it is that unique ability to project into the future, that makes us so successful as a race.

How many times has the long-term outcome of a decision been in the forefront of our minds when we are making it? Sometimes we forget to consider the very long-term outcomes and just go with our heart. That can work of course, but isn't always the wisest route to take. Ideally, we should consider our head as well. The two will help us even more.

In practical terms, it is impossible to predict precisely the outcome of anything we do. But it is more predictable than we think. The outcomes are always different but the path is often a repeated one; the chances are that someone else somewhere has done what you are about to do.

If, before you make the decision, you can somehow get your head around researching it and finding out what others did in your situation, and then act on it, you will have the wisdom to make your accumulated effort more in line with what you truly want. Going back to the example of joining a gym, being able to run a marathon and have a BMI of 20 percent may impact on other areas that are costly. Time sacrifice, relationship compromise, money issues and so on.

There are so many lessons out there that people have recorded and want you to read so you don't make the same mistakes. Almost every biography has a warning in it. They will likely also have some suggestions. Do not ignore them.

Let's take a view of your life over the next week. Easy! Not too many surprises usually. One month, takes a bit of consideration; you will find there are projects that you know you should be working on but are not yet doing so. This reflection starts to open your opinion of what's important. Now, consider going forward a year and you start to feel unable to make predictions too accurately and it feels too long a time period to get any sense of urgency.

Five years seems a ridiculous period to consider. Ten, almost no one does. Twenty and you'll get laughed at if you share it or consider it next time you put your head on the pillow. Here is an example that Patricia shared with me when helping me edit my work:

> *I have actually used the five year test nearly all of my life. Not quite in the way that you mention, but turning it around. I would say: Okay, in five years' time where do I want to be, where do I want to have visited, what do I want to own? I would draw up a five year Bucket List: I want to have done this, I want to own that, I want to have gone there. Most importantly, I do not want to be here, stagnating! That is, in the same situation having made no progress. So then I would ask myself, if I want to achieve these things, what have I got to do NOW to ensure that any or all of those things happen? It is by*

instigating change! I have made some drastic changes in my life to ensure I wasn't in the same situation five years hence. I suspect it comes from deep-rooted fear of not having enough time to complete my Life's Bucket List. Interestingly, I heard many years later, an American self-help motivator enthusing over the five year plan....

Here's how to deal with this. Each decision made in the now will have a long-term effect that you can consider to predict. It allows you to transport your thinking over time in a way that guessing and trying to predict without that reference point will not. Being proactive rather than reactive.

Let's take having puddings with your meals out. You know that repeated over the next 25 years it will make you heavier than if you abstained. That in turn makes you unable to do many things that you might otherwise have done; maybe take up golf when you retire or running to keep fit, or just being active with the grandchildren. You could almost assume that the puddings will lead to a health problem with maybe your heart, blood pressure or diabetes.

My point is this: it is so much easier when you focus first on the action and then on the long-term effects 25 years ahead and try to live accordingly.

The next view is almost the opposite but with a subtle difference. If you wanted to ensure that your heart rate was healthy in old age you could decide with your doctor rather than work out what to do over the next 25 years and then, working backwards, make the decisions today that support that plan. Cut out puddings! Take up running, take up golf. NOW! It's not rocket science is it? This reflects Patricia's outlook.

It still all boils down to what you decide today. With the thought first in mind that you have the choice, almost always, and if you weigh it up with the fact that a spoonful of sugar becomes a mountain before too long, it changes how you react to the choice of sponge pudding and custard.

In no way will you be able to become fully active in all your decisions from day one. Outside influences hinder this. People, marketing, group dynamics, your state of mind at the time of making the decision and much more will all have a bearing.

Your key to making a change is what tools you have at your disposal when you make the decision. One I am sure you won't yet have developed is your accumulation thought process.

So here's a question to carry around with you for the rest of your life. It is your friend. It will make a massive difference if you will just use it each time you make a decision that is important.

What are the long-term effects of this decision?

In other words, clog or cleanse? Teach or taunt? Build or break?

How else are you ever going to be able to get a grip on your bad habits or even the one-offs that change your life? How else can you find the momentum that makes you excited about what you choose to do on a daily basis?

Decisions can be big or small: contemplate divorce, save money, buy that dress or whether to have a dog. Some have more far-reaching consequences than others, but maybe not.

That sexy dress could attract the love of your life. That dog could cause you to walk every day and get fit enough to make old age great. That £100 per month into the stock market could be what helps you buy that dream home. That divorce could turn you into a street dweller.

By keeping this question in mind it helps in every area no matter how small. It is a practical solution to your life's outcome because it makes you think: **Cause** and **Effect.**

Life will present many problems and opportunities to you. Sometimes you'll have such a run of bad luck you'll think the one upstairs has got it in for you. Here's what you can rely on though. You'll become a product of your decisions. All those decisions that you made in the past are with you now. Go back ten years and have a chat with yourself in your imagination. I will bet you'll tell yourself to make some different decisions.

It is fun to imagine having a talk with your past self. It is fun to also assume you are talking to your future self and asking for advice and letting the answers come to you. The hard part is acting on it. Only you can do that.

It's your life. You might as well make it a good one. Doc Brown said that in *Back to the Future.*

What are the long-term effects of this action?

Use the future test to your advantage. Patricia's version is a reflection on where she wants to be in five years' time. Her future test helps her reflect on the decisions that move her towards her goals or something that takes her away from it. We are all motivated by something external as well as internal. We all prefer to be motivated in different ways. Some by avoiding pain or embarrassment, some by the desire for something better. Tune in to your internal guidance system. "Let your soul be your pilot," sang Sting.

> *"Lost time is never found again."*
>
> *Benjamin Franklin*

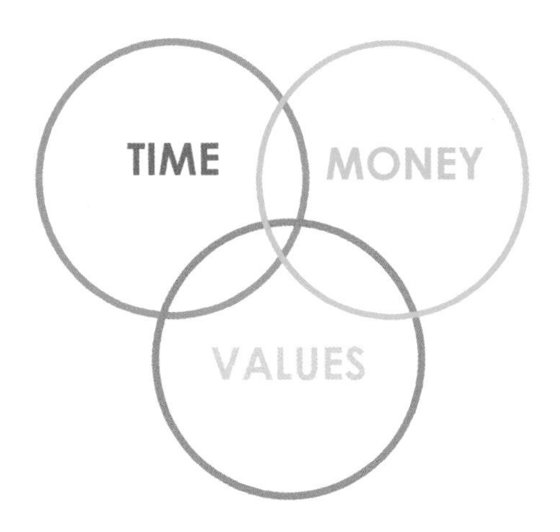

Always seek to find your balance between these three.

Being Practical

1. Make a list of all the things you spend time on. Anything and everything. From cleaning your shoes to building your dream home. Decide which of those activities you could get someone else to do easily, especially the ones you detest doing. You will free up a whole bunch of time, very quickly.

2. Decide how best to use this new time for the positive, keeping in mind the long-term outcome of the decisions and activities.

3. Share your thinking with a mentor or significant other for clarity and perspective.

Overview

There are seven parts to this book and each part contains some ideas that relate to the subject. I have chosen big enough subjects to focus on at the start of using this process. It is not a limit of topics to use this concept for. The concept can be used on anything you choose.

The seven areas are:

HEALTH

YOUR EDUCATION

MONEY

RELATIONSHIPS

YOUR SPIRITUAL THINKING AND VALUES

BEING AT PEACE

YOUR TIME

Just by paying positive attention to these, you will improve so many areas of your life that it may be enough. I, of course, will want to encourage you to reach out much further. Examples could be your community, how you help others, and many more.

Please let your creative juices flow. We are amazing. What we can do is amazing.

Space around these images have been left for you to make your own notes as you read and capture your thoughts.

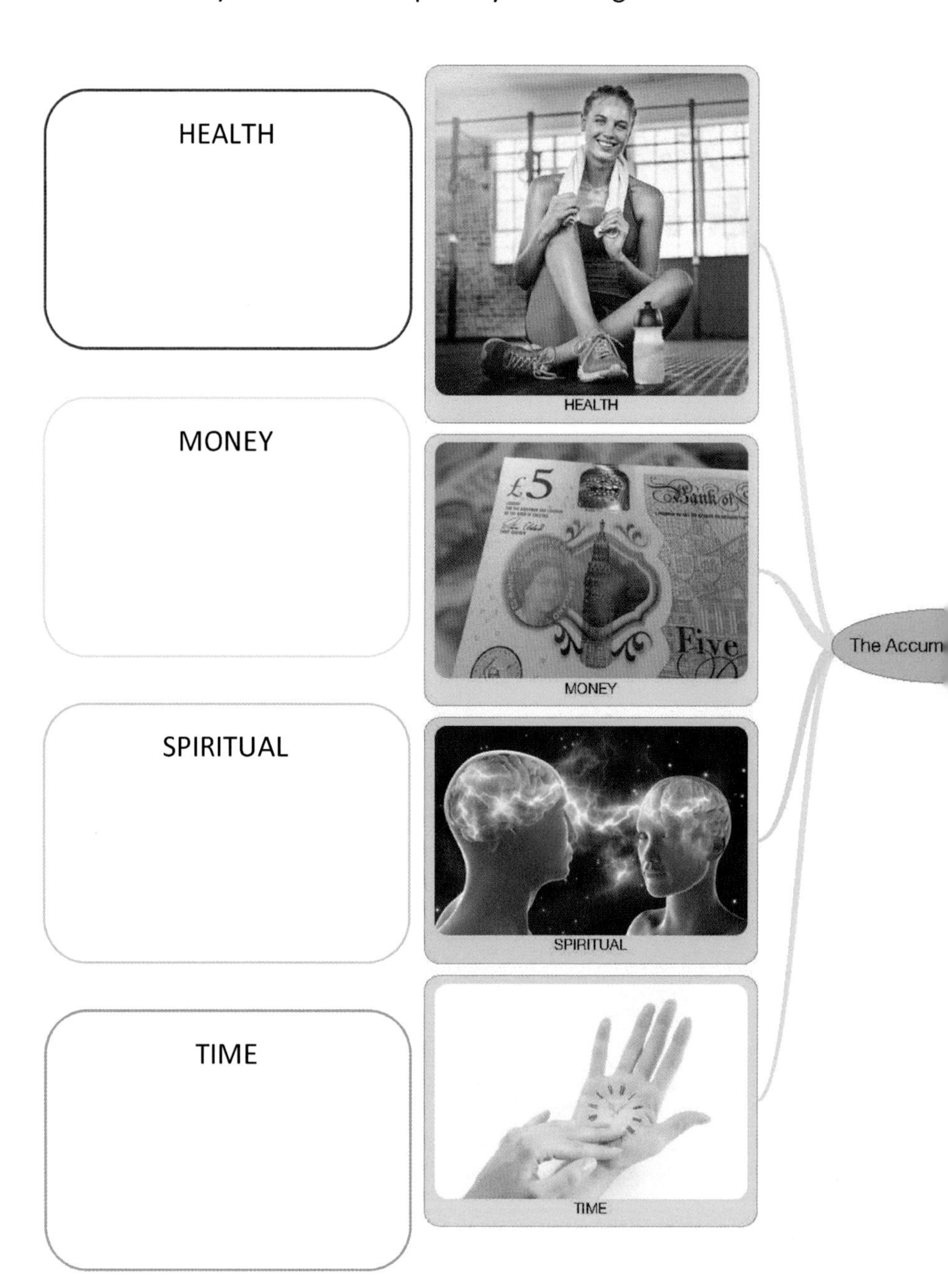

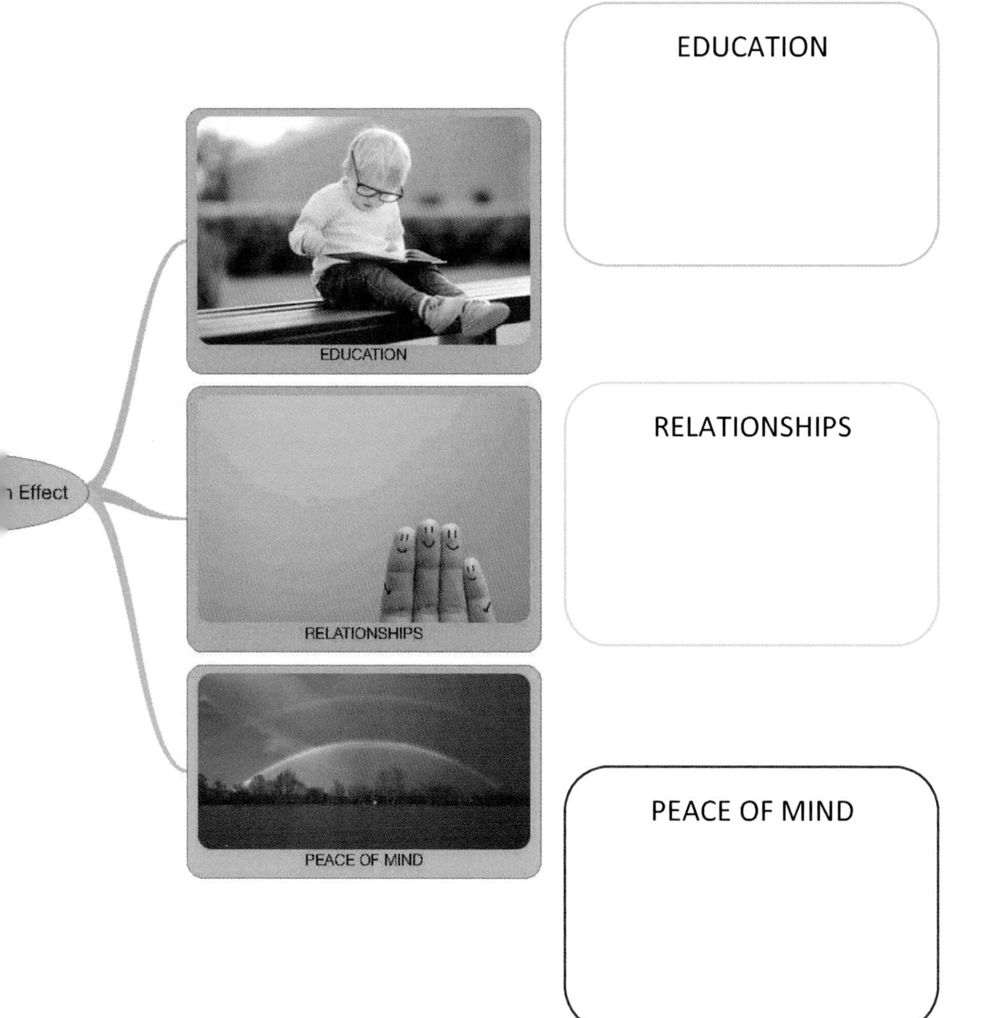
EDUCATION
Effect
EDUCATION
RELATIONSHIPS
RELATIONSHIPS
PEACE OF MIND
PEACE OF MIND

My Challenge to You

I have tools in my businesses and the guidance of myself that serve me well. My hope is that you will share this wisdom and that you will add to it by submitting your own ideas to:

ideas@theaccumulationeffect.com

Help me build a bigger and better version of this over the years ahead.

I want to share and accumulate this style of thinking to benefit as many people as I can. I challenge you therefore to expand your thinking and a first step is to ask you to submit a story that has an accumulation effect lesson that you consider will to be useful to others.

Good luck with all your plans and futures.

Thank you for taking the time to read this book.

Stephen

If you want to know more about Stephen and his related businesses, please visit www.stephenaoliver.com

About the Author

Stephen lives in Northampton with his wife Tracey and two daughters. They met working together.

Having worked for Standard Chartered Bank, Debenhams and a Mortgage Broker, he decided to train as a financial adviser in 1990. He has grown many businesses and passionately enjoys coaching.

Motorcycling, scuba diving, travelling, reading and having studied neuro linguistic programming make Stephen very experienced. This has taught him we can all benefit from the experiences of others. He believes sharing and coaching enhances what we are to each other. Being willing to share and give, helps bring out the happier side of us in many ways.

Financially independent, looking to contribute to and develop others as well as teach what works, he tends to focus on progress not shortfalls. He knows it makes us happier, develops enthusiasm and our motivation.

Jim Rohn and Stephen R. Covey are personal development favourites of his. Although they both died recently, they left a legacy of helping people be the best they can be. He hopes to emulate them and feels it would make good use of his life.

He refuses to let age slow him down. Having a spinal operation in 2006 he understands the need for a healthy body. Knowing your weaknesses gives strength. At 6' 2" he is keen to keep his mobility which he nearly lost.

"Being happy productive and fit takes effort and sometimes a big change of thinking. Making a tiny shift can significantly enhance your life. That must be worth searching for", says Stephen.

"I want to give something back for those that have given to me, in the hope that those who receive what I give will pass that on too. Holding on to your gifts or knowledge is ineffective and wasteful. Please make 1 plus 1 equal as much as possible.

Pleasure for me comes from doing what I love. What you and I see are often different views of the same thing. Sharing our views helps us grow, and accumulated knowledge makes the growth magnificent."